AN EYEWITNESS BOOK

The Printer and his Craft

HELEN WODZICKA

WAYLAND PUBLISHERS

More Eyewitness Books

Frontispiece: A sixteenth century printing office.

SBN 85340 175 6

Copyright © 1972 by
Wayland Publishers Limited

First published in 1972 by
Wayland Publishers Limited
49 Lansdowne Place, Hove, East Sussex BN3 1HF
Second impression 1978

Reproduced and printed by photolithography and bound in
Great Britain at The Pitman Press, Bath

CONTENTS

THE INVENTION OF PRINTING

One of the first things we learn at school is reading. Long ago, before printing was invented, most people could not read at all. Few people had books of their own. Today, books are cheap enough for everyone to buy. Schools teach everyone to read. It has not always been like this. Printing made it possible.

From the earliest times men have wanted to record their thoughts. Cave men scratched on tree-bark or bone. The ancient Assyrians carved on clay tablets and stone. The ancient Egyptians wrote on *papyrus*. The Greeks and Romans wrote on papyrus, and on *parchment* too. The early Christian monks of England and Ireland wrote their copies of the Gospels on parchment.

As you can guess, all these ways of writing were slow. Also, stone, papyrus and parchment were costly materials. They were also rather a nuisance to carry around. A book is a lot handier than a block of stone. In the *Middle Ages* there were few books and not many people could read. Most of the teachers were church-men, and they taught only the clergy, lawyers and a few rich men.

Printing was invented in the mid 15th century in Germany, about the time of the Wars of the Roses in England. Within fifty years printing had spread to other countries in Europe. It also spread to the New World where Christopher Columbus first sailed in the year 1492. But many years passed before books could be made cheaply. As you read on, you will see how the demand for education and books grew side by side.

CLAY TABLETS. Look at this ancient clay tablet, with a map of the world carved on it. The letters tell us about the conquests of King Sargon of Agade who ruled in Babylon about 2300 B.C. The Babylonians, Assyrians, and Romans recorded their histories by cutting them into clay and stone. It was slow work, but tablets lasted a long time. The ancient peoples could have easily made a printing press. But they had many slaves to cut the clay and stone tablets, so perhaps they never even thought about it.

PAPYRUS. The ancient Egyptians wrote with simple pictures instead of letters. This picture-writing was called *hieroglyphics*. About 3,000 years ago the Egyptians wrote on papyrus. You can see it in the above right-hand picture. It was made from the pith, or soft inside of reeds growing in the River Nile. Strips of pith were pasted over each other in layers, and dried in the hot sun. The Egyptians, Greeks and Romans used papyrus. It is no good for making into books, as it cannot be folded—only rolled up. The picture opposite shows rolls of papyrus in a Roman library about the time of Christ.

SCRIBES. In the Middle Ages, monks copied out by
hand all the Gospels, and Greek and Roman learning.
You can imagine what a long slow task this must have
been. These hand-copied books are called *manuscripts*.
The monks are known as *scribes* which comes from the
Latin "to write." The scribes also decorated the books
with pictures in beautiful colours. Since there were few
books—many of them beautiful—they were very
precious objects. In many museums you can still see
some of these rare manuscripts.

MONASTERIES AND EDUCATION. This picture shows a monk teaching grammar in the late Middle Ages. In England the monks taught the clergy, lawyers, and rich men until Henry VIII closed all the monasteries down in 1534. Monks did most of the teaching because they had many books. Look back at the picture of the scribe, and notice how thick and heavy his manuscripts are. They were not meant to be moved around much; they were kept in the monasteries for the monks and for teaching.

PARCHMENT. Manuscripts were copied out on specially prepared animal skins. The skins were given a smooth white surface. They came from young sheep and calves butchered in the autumn for eating. The meat was salted and preserved for the winter; the skins were prepared by craftsmen and sent to the monasteries. The skins were called parchment, or *vellum*, and they were very expensive. Here a craftsman is preparing some parchment. He has stretched the skins out on frames, and is now damping them so that they will shrink and dry flat. He will scrub them white and smooth with pumice stone or chalk.

PAPER. The Spanish were the first Europeans to make paper, about the time of the first Crusade. Paper mills were later set up in other countries. In this picture, you can see a watermill through the back window. The mill turned hammers which beat rags into separate bits. These bits of rag were put into a vat of water, and a wire tray—called a paper mould—was dipped in. The bits of rag which stuck to the mould were dried between pieces of felt. The result was paper. It was much cheaper to make than parchment.

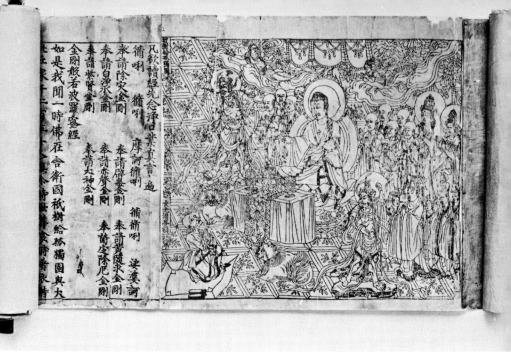

BLOCK PRINTING. As we have seen, copying pictures and text by hand was slow and costly. Printing is a way of making many copies of a page at the same time. The earliest form of printing was done with wooden blocks. The printer made a picture or letters on wood by cutting away the background. Then he inked the raised surface, and pressed a piece of paper on top of it. The same block could be used many times. It is just like printing from a lino cut or a potato. The Chinese made the scroll above in 868, almost 200 years before the Battle of Hastings.

WOODBLOCK PLAYING CARDS. In the Middle Ages, printers used wood blocks to make playing cards and religious pictures. As they were printed on paper, almost everyone could afford them. They were simple pictures with very few words. Most people, remember, could not read. You can see these cards in the picture opposite. The picture above them shows a blockmaker at work.

14

PRINTING PRESSES. The picture above shows a French printing office about the time of Gutenberg. Notice the press in the middle of the room. Early presses were built of wood; the printer turned the large screw to press the paper onto the inked type. On the right, a bookseller is selling finished books. Gutenberg's office would have looked rather like it. The first printers sold their own books from their offices. The picture is from a set called the "Dance of Death." The skeletons are Death coming to the printers. Sudden death was very real to the people of the Middle Ages because of war, famine, and plague.

JOHANN GUTENBERG. Johann Gutenberg was a goldsmith who lived in Germany long ago. In 1429 he invented a way of printing words using moveable pieces of *type*. These were separate letters of type which can be fitted together as words, and put into a press for printing. Afterwards, the letters can be split up and used again to print something else. This kind of printing is called *letterpress* printing. Gutenberg's printed books were very beautiful. He made them look like hand-written manuscripts because his customers were used to this style.

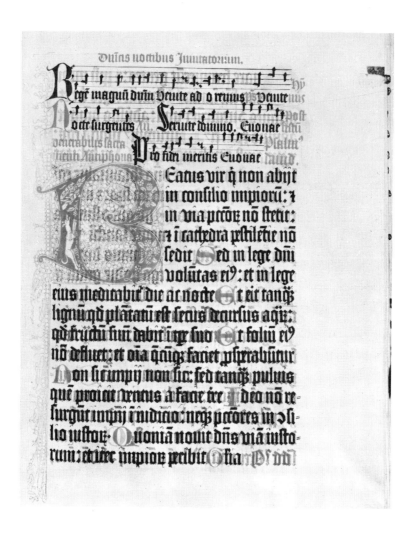

THE BLACK ART. Gutenberg's partner, a man named Fust, printed this Psalter, or prayer book, in 1457. If you look at the scribe on page 10, you will see that his manuscript looked very much like this printed book. The larger initials in this prayer book were drawn by hand. Fust was nearly arrested for witchcraft when he published it. People did not believe it was printed; they thought it was an invention of the Devil. Printing was often called "The Black Art" for this reason. Printers' apprentices were called "devils" or "imps".

WILLIAM CAXTON. William Caxton was a London businessman who translated and printed the first book in English about 1473. This picture shows him giving a book to King Edward IV. Caxton printed books for the Church. He also printed books to be read for pleasure. Geoffrey Chaucer's *Canterbury Tales* was printed by Caxton in 1478 and 1484. It had to be printed twice—it was so popular that it sold out the first time. Caxton advertised his books and sold them quite cheaply.

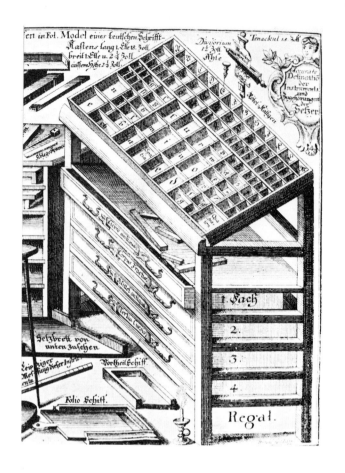

20

COMPOSITORS. The printers who put separate pieces of type together into words are called *compositors* and their job is called composing. The pieces of type were kept in a special case like the one on the left. Notice that the types are not kept in alphabetical order but in order of use. There are big compartments for common letters like, a, e, i, o, u. Two compositors in the picture below it take letters from the cases. They make the letters up into words and sentences, and put them in the sticks which they hold. Then they will transfer the letters to a tray and clamp it on the press ready for printing.

TYPE. Below is a piece of printing from the time of Gutenberg and Caxton. Remember that each letter was printed from one piece of type. Notice that two letters are sometimes joined. They were called *ligatures*; printers used them to save time. You can also see that a piece of type has fallen over sideways by accident. The letters look very strange to us today. How many can you read? This type is called "Gothic", or black-letter type.

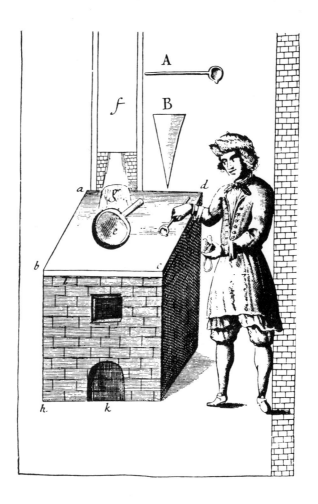

TYPEFOUNDING. Typefounders made the little pieces of type; it was a very skilled craft. Early printers cast their own type. They heated a mixture of lead and tin in an oven like the one in the picture. Then they poured the hot metal very carefully into a *mould*. The typefounder here holds a mould in his left hand. He will open the mould when the metal has cooled. Then he will remove the type, and smooth it with a file.

ILLUSTRATED BOOKS. The titlepage of this book was printed in Italy about 500 years ago. It has pictures and text together. Woodblocks and type could be printed together in the same press. The press would have looked like the one in the centre picture. The type and the blocks were locked into place. They were inked and paper placed on top. The printer screwed the paper onto the blocks and type to make an *impression*.

BOOKBINDING. Early printers bound up their books in strong leather. They often decorated the binding with the coat of arms of the nobleman who bought the book. This picture shows bookbinders at work. The man at the back is sorting out the pages of a book ready for binding. The other man is trimming the tops of the pages inside the book so that it will look tidy.

PUBLISHERS. To "publish" means to make known. A publisher today works with the author, has the books printed, and sends them to booksellers who sell them to the public. In Caxton's day most printers acted as publishers and booksellers as well. The picture shows one of the first real publishers. His main job was to send books to the people who had bought them. He is packing the books in a barrel so that they can be shipped safely.

PRINTERS' MARKS. These pictures are "marks" used by the early printers and publishers. They showed who made the book even if people could not read. Often the pictures were jokes or puns on the name of the printer, so that people would remember it more easily. Publishers still have their own marks today. If you look at the title page of this book you will see the mark that Wayland Publishers use.

LIBRARIES. The opposite picture shows a library in the time of Henry VIII. Notice how the valuable books have been chained to the shelves to stop people stealing them. Libraries were first started in monasteries and universities. The picture above it shows a medieval university. Libraries and universities grew rapidly in the 15th and 16th centuries. This period was known as the *Renaissance*, which means rebirth. It was a wonderful time of progress in art, buildings, printing, books and learning. Printed books helped to spread the new learning.

28

CRAFT TO TECHNOLOGY

The Renaissance was a "rebirth" of curiosity about the world, and a new interest in learning. All sorts of new discoveries were made by scientists and inventors, doctors and explorers. People had new ideas about religion, politics and education. Printing helped all this, because people could read about the new ideas in books and pamphlets. Printing recorded all these changes.

Printing and publishing grew to suit the rising number of people who could read. More people were going to school, and learning to read and write. Not only the very rich, but members of the prosperous middle class—the merchants and master-craftsmen—could now afford to buy books.

Many technical changes took place in printing as time passed. New machines took the place of jobs done by hand. These machines could print much faster and more cheaply. Printing offices were no longer small craftsmen's workshops; they became big noisy factories. This happened in other industries like weaving and pottery. We call this time of change the *Industrial Revolution*.

Few poor people and countryfolk owned much more than a Bible and one or two other books. Instead of reading, they would tell one another stories by the fireside in their spare time. Many of them could not read at all, and could never afford books for pleasure.

SCHOOLS. Here is an English school during the reign of James I, about 1610. Notice that only the teacher has a book. His eight pupils are writing on slates. Children used slates until the 20th century, because paper cost far too much for schoolbooks. The first children's schoolbooks were made from stiff sheets of animal horn; these lasted a long time. In the 17th century, more schools were opened in the villages, and more grammar schools were founded for the sons of the wealthy. Even so, most children never went to school at all.

BOOKSELLERS. This bookseller's shop was probably part of a printer's office. Look at the books behind the reading table: they have been put on the shelf backwards. This was usual until printers began to print the titles on the spines. The famous diarist Samuel Pepys was one of the first to have titles on his books. He had a library of 3,000 books, a huge collection for his time. Few people had more than one or two books so titles were not needed. Booksellers used to lend books to their trusted customers. If the customer liked the book, he would buy it.

NEWS SHEETS. Early newspapers were called "news sheets." They were printed all through the English Civil War. Unlike today's daily papers, news sheets were not issued at fixed times. They told people about the fighting between Charles I and the Cavaliers, and Parliament and the Roundheads. They were printed by both sides. Pictures of current events were very popular. These pictures show Charles I in prison on the Isle of Wight and his beheading in London in 1649. Oliver Cromwell had some news sheets specially reprinted for his army in Scotland, so that they would not feel out of touch.

PEDLARS. Here is a pedlar selling news sheets. From the Middle Ages, pedlars tramped around the country-side selling their wares. This pedlar would also sell copies of hymns or ballads and religious pictures. It was often the only way village folk could get anything to read at all. With no television, radio or telephones, they needed these little pieces of printing for contact with the outside world.

ALMANACS. Some wandering pedlars sold almanacs. These were little books which had a calendar, and the dates of all the festivals and holidays. The writer of the almanac would tell of future events which he had seen in the stars. Countryfolk who were unable to read could at least enjoy the pictures. Notice the sheet of paper hanging from the pedlar's tray—it is a wall calendar.

PRINTING THE BIBLE. During Henry VIII's reign (1509–47), printers began to publish the Latin Bible in English. Until then only churchmen, lawyers and scholars who knew Latin could read the Bible. Ordinary people in England wanted to read the Bible in their own language so that they could understand it. The printer in this picture is giving Henry VIII a copy of the first English Bible.

PUNISHMENTS. In Tudor times hundreds of people in England and on the Continent were burned at the stake for refusing to obey the Church. Printers were jailed or sent to the stake for printing books which the authorities had banned. The authorities made bonfires of their books. Books were thought to be dangerous because they let people think for themselves. When printers heard they were going to be arrested, they often fled to other countries and set up new presses.

STAR CHAMBER. The picture opposite is a London printing office at the time of James I (1603–25). The government fixed the number of printing offices in order to control what was printed. It was afraid that people would read books and pamphlets criticizing the government and Church. This law was enforced by a special court called the Star Chamber. If a printer disobeyed the Star Chamber, an official would take away his printing equipment to stop him working.

A
DECREE
Concerning OF *Printing etc.*
Starre-Chamber,
CONCERNING
PRINTING,

Made the eleuenth day of July last past. 1 6 3 7.

DIEV ET MON DROIT.

❡ Imprinted at London by *Robert Barker,*
Printer to the Kings most Excellent
Maiestie: And by the Assignes
of *Iohn Bill.* 1 6 3 7.

MASTER-PRINTER'S OFFICE. The large office below belongs to a Dutch master-printer of the 1670's. The men working the press are *journeymen*. They have finished their training and now work for master-printers. They are hired and paid by the day. The apprentice above would join a master-printer's office to learn the trade. He would do all the odd jobs. He is carrying the ink balls for inking the metal type, as well beer and pies for his master!

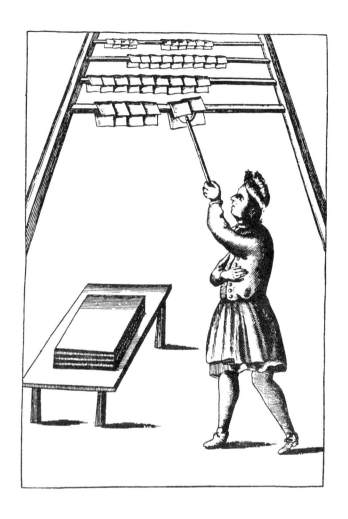

PRINTERS' TEXTBOOK. This picture comes from the first textbook of printing. The book was published in two parts. Publishers did this so that the sales of Part One would pay for Part Two. This picture shows a printer how to hang up the wet printed sheets to dry. Damp paper was used for printing. This made the paper softer and the metal type would "bite" better and make a good sharp impression.

PRINTERS' CUSTOMS. This picture shows the famous American patriot Benjamin Franklin (1706–90) when he worked in a London printing office. People said that he was so disgusted with the drunken English printers that he refused to mix with them. They teased him by hiding his tools and type until he joined in with them. This was called "being haunted by the chapel ghost." *Chapel* was the name for a group of printers who worked together. Maybe he then agreed to go with the printers on their annual outing, or wayz-goose. Before he left Franklin had them all drinking milk—or so he believed.

PRINTING IN AMERICA. Stephen Daye, an English settler, set up the first printing press in America in the 17th century. The American people wanted to read many books, pamphlets, and news sheets. Colonial printers helped to spread ideas which led to the American Revolution of 1776. They printed a pamphlet called *Common Sense* which was written by Tom Paine, who you see above. The pamphlet urged the Colonies to break with George III and England. *Common Sense* was a best-seller—one copy was sold for every twenty-five people in America.

PRINTING SHAKESPEARE. Here is one of William Shakespeare's plays being performed in the reign of Charles II (1660–85). People who went to Shakespeare's plays also wanted to read them. The picture opposite is the title-page of the first *edition* of Shakespeare's plays. It was called the "First Folio." *Folio* is the name for a book with very large pages.

Mr. WILLIAM
SHAKESPEARES

COMEDIES,
HISTORIES, &
TRAGEDIES.

Published according to the True Originall Copies.

Martin Droeshout sculpsit London.

LONDON

Printed by Isaac Iaggard, and Ed. Blount. 1623.

PRINTING THE CLASSICS. Many years ago, boys from rich families learned Greek and Latin at grammar schools. Later, they made a "grand tour" of Europe, especially Italy and Greece, as part of their education. You can see visitors to Rome in the picture above. Educated men wanted copies of Greek and Roman texts, such as Homer, Cicero and Virgil. This new demand was met by John Baskerville (1706–75). He was a writing master in Birmingham, and an engraver of gravestones, before he became a printer. He cut new letters and made his own type moulds, presses, and ink. His beautiful type, shown opposite, was named after him. If you compare it with the type on page 21 you will see how much easier it is to read. It is still popular today.

D. JUNII

JUVENALIS

ET

AULI

PERSII FLACCI

SATYRAE.

BIRMINGHAMIAE:

Typis JOHANNIS BASKERVILLE.

MDCCLXI.

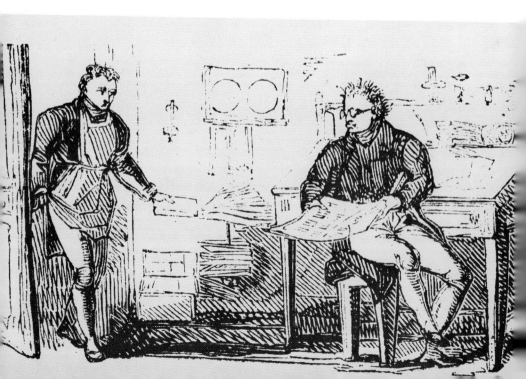

NEWSPAPERS. The first newspapers were published in the 18th century. They were very heavily taxed, so that the government could stop too many people reading them. Few people could afford to buy them. One newspaper was passed from hand to hand. People often met in coffee-houses, like the one above, to read a newspaper and to talk about current affairs.

READERS. Look at the pictures on the left. Above, a master-printer is telling his journeymen and apprentice what to do. The man at the back is correcting a *proof* of the finished page. Standing next to him is the author, who has come to help. Authors used to correct the proofs in the printing office, but they got in the way of the printers. Printers preferred to employ separate people as correctors. They are called "readers." You can see one on the left.

AUTHORS. Here an author shows his new manuscript to a publisher, who does not seem to think much of it. In the 18th century authors were given a legal right to own what they had written. This is called the copyright. Henry Fielding was a very popular author; his publisher paid him £1,000 in 1761 for writing his novel *Amelia*. Five thousand copies were sold in under a week. This was a huge number when we think that the cheapest novel cost more than most men earned in a week.

PUBLISHERS. This is the portrait of a leading publisher and bookseller, Jacob Tonson. He lived in the time of Queen Anne (1702–14) and his firm published the works of some of our greatest writers like William Shakespeare, John Dryden, and John Milton. He died leaving £80,000 which was a fortune in those days. But publishing was still a risky business, so many publishers were booksellers as well.

AUCTIONS. Here is a book auction at Christie's in the 18th century. Christie's is still a very famous London auction room. As you can see, the firm started in quite a simple way. In an auction, people bid higher and higher prices for an object and the highest offer gets it. Books sold by auction are usually antiquarian books, which means old, rare and valuable.

STANHOPE PRESS. In 1803, Earl Stanhope invented an iron printing press which was named after him. Two other iron presses followed it, the Columbian and the Albion. Iron presses were not very different from wooden ones, but they were stronger and could print twice as fast. They were an example of the new technical improvements of the Industrial Revolution.

IRON PRESSES. The picture above shows printers at work about 1820. The iron press they are using is a Columbian. Its American inventor used an American eagle for one of the counterweights, which worked the screw of the press. Notice the large area which the machines can print. The man is inking the type with a new kind of roller, instead of dabbing it with old-fashioned ink balls. Rollers were another invention of the Industrial Revolution. But one man is still composing the words by hand, and another is hanging up wet sheets one by one to dry.

FACTORY PRINTING. This 19th century printing works on the right has none of the simple atmosphere of the old master-printer's shop. The men are working huge, fast and noisy machines, which are driven by steam engines. Notice how large this room is and how few windows it has. Gas lighting was used, and printers had to work long after sunset.

POPULAR PRINTING

The new printing machinery invented during the Industrial Revolution meant that books and newspapers could be printed much faster and more cheaply. At the same time, more and more people were going to school and learning to read. In 1870 an important Education Act was passed in England. Every child now had to attend primary school. For the first time, children from poor working families, and from the farms, had the chance to learn to read. People saw that children would enjoy reading if they had interesting books specially written for them. The first popular children's books were published about this time. Adults, too, could educate themselves. Adult education centres were set up. They were called Mechanics' Institutes, or Working Men's Colleges. They were the beginning of today's Polytechnics.

People have always wanted to read for fun. Then, as now, people liked reading about romance, scandal and murders. There was a growing demand for books, magazines and newspapers of every kind. In 1850, public libraries were set up in England. Now everyone, not just the privileged could read anything they wanted— free of charge.

SUNDAY SCHOOLS. Sunday schools were started by a newspaper owner, Robert Raikes, in 1780. The schools tried to teach children to read so that they could understand the Scriptures. But children who had to work long hours in factories or coal mines did not enjoy going to school on their day off. When very poor children could not find work, they went to "ragged schools" like the one in the opposite picture below. These schools were run by charities. They had very few books and did not teach many children to read.

SCHOOLS. The picture below shows a schoolroom after the Education Act had been passed in 1870. Compare this school with the ragged school on the opposite page. Certainly these children are much better off. They each have a book of their own. Notice that two teachers are giving lessons in the same room.

CHILDREN'S BOOKS. Children all through the ages have liked fairy stories and adventure stories. But not many exciting stories were published for children until the time of Queen Victoria (1837–1901). Parents and teachers saw that children would enjoy reading if they had books specially written for them. Children's books now had pictures in them. You can see one of these above. Below, a boy and girl are buying books at a children's book shop.

BOY'S OWN PAPER. Children's magazines also became very popular. *The Boy's Own Magazine, Boy's Own Journal* and *Penny Magazine* are just some of them. Copies were often coloured by hand after printing, to make them more exciting. Some magazines printed very blood-thirsty adventure stories. The Religious Tract Society thought they could be very harmful to children. In 1879, the Society began to publish its own magazine, the *Boy's Own Paper*. It was very successful. Jules Verne and Conan Doyle, the creator of Sherlock Holmes, wrote stories for it.

No. 1.—Vol. I.   SATURDAY, JANUARY 18, 1879.   Price One Penny.
[ALL RIGHTS RESERVED.]

MY FIRST FOOTBALL MATCH.

BY AN OLD BOY.

IT was a proud moment in my existence when Wright, captain of our football club, came up to me in school one Friday and said, "Adams, your name is down to play in the match against Craven to-morrow."

I could have knighted him on the spot. To be one of the picked "fifteen," whose glory it was to fight the battles of their school in the Great Close, had been the leading ambition of my life—I suppose I ought to be ashamed to confess it—ever since, as a little chap of ten, I entered Parkhurst six years ago. Not a winter Saturday but had seen me either looking on at some big match, or oftener still scrimmaging about with a score or so of other juniors in a scratch game. But for a long time, do what I would, I always

seemed as far as ever from the coveted goal, and was half despairing of ever rising to win my "first fifteen cap." Latterly, however, I had noticed Wright and a few others of our best players more than once lounging about in the Little Close where we juniors used to play, evidently taking observations with an eye to business. Under the awful gaze of these heroes, need I say I exerted myself as I had never done before? What cared I for hacks or bruises, so only that I could distinguish myself in their eyes? And never was music sweeter

MECHANICS' INSTITUTES. Children were not the only ones with more chance to read. In Queen Victoria's time, adults could go to evening schools called Mechanics' Institutes. Here they could study reading, engineering, and science. Later, the Institutes became social centres as well. Libraries, drama societies and reading groups were started. This picture shows the novelist Charles Dickens (1812—70) reading from one of his books to a Mechanics' Institute meeting.

THE HA'PENNY REVOLUTION. As we saw, most people could not afford newspapers because of the heavy tax. As more people learned to read, they wanted to buy newspapers of their own. They made such a fuss about the tax that the government abolished it in 1855. Now, many popular newspapers could be printed. This was often called the "Ha'Penny Revolution," because that is what the newspapers cost. The picture shows a busy newspaper office trying to cope with all the extra work.

THE *TIMES*. The *Times* was always an important newspaper. Above, carts are collecting copies of the paper for the morning delivery. Morning papers are printed during the night so they can be on the news stands as people go to work. The *Times* had a great influence on the thoughts and actions of English people.

PRINTING MACHINES. The newspaper press at the top of the opposite page is called a 10-feeder because ten men could feed paper into it at once. The type is on the cylinder in the middle of the machine. Notice the ten rollers which ink the type. The *Times* installed this machine in 1861 to meet the growing demands from its readers. It could print a thousand sheets an hour, but only one side of the page. The opposite picture shows a printing press called the 8-feeder.

ROTARY PRESSES. This is the printing office of the *Illustrated London News* in 1879. The men on the right are working *rotary presses*. The paper was fed through the cylinders and could be printed on both sides at once. This is called *perfecting*. Rotary presses did much to boost newspaper circulation because they could print so much faster than the old 10-feeders.

TYPESETTING. As we have seen, composing type by hand was a very slow and skilled trade. Inventors worked hard on a machine to do the job. The machine in this picture was called the Kastenbein typesetter. Instead of picking up each tiny letter by hand, the typesetter just tapped the letters he wanted, like a typewriter. The machine also sorted out the letters after they had been used, so they could be used again. The *Times* installed this typesetter in the 1870's.

MAGAZINES. These people are eagerly reading the *Graphic* magazine at an exhibition in Paris. Magazines had been taxed like newspapers, but when this tax was taken off, many different kinds of magazines were published—for children, for women and home interests, for hobbies, and for current events. The machines that printed newspapers and magazines were the most advanced in the printing industry. Printing was fast and cheap, but the quality was not very high. Good paper, good ink, and careful hand work had been pushed aside for the sake of cheapness and speed.

CATNACH. James Catnach and other printers became famous for printing gruesome accounts of murders, scandals and sporting events. These subjects were as popular in the past as they are today. People liked to read about the last words of a man before he was executed. Catnach often printed the same "famous last words" again and again. Boys known as "running patterers" sold these scandal sheets on the streets.

ACCOUNT OF THE GREAT

FIGHT

BETWEEN

J. Heenan & T. King

For Two Thousand Pounds.

being the day appointed to decide the great fight
etween Jack Heenan and Tom King, the men, accom-
anied by their respective backers and a select number of
riends, started at an early hour by train, which had been
pecially engaged for the occasion Having gone some
i-tance down the line, they alighted, and made their way
o the spot selected for the great contest

THE FIGHT.

Round 1.—When the men faced each other there was
ot such a contrast as we have seen on former occasions.
Heenan is much stouter than when he appeared in the
ing with Tom Sayers; and, in fact, looked in excellent
ondition He had evidently made up his mind to win.
While King, who was equally as confident, looked in
rst-rate health. We must say every attention has been
aid to their training, and gives much credit to their
espective trainers. A great deal of sparring took place
r an opening, at length Heenan let fly, and caught
King on the mug, and got away. King followed up
Heenan, in retreat, told again with the left, and planted
stinger on the ivories. More sparring and counter hits
ow took place. In the close both were down.

2.—Heenan led off with the right, but fell short. The
ext attempt was better, hitting King on the left peeper,
rawing the claret most freely—first blood for Heenan.
ter a few smart exchanges King was fought down.

—Time being called, Heenan was first to the scratch.
ing now began to look flushed. Heenan was the first to
ash out, planting his right on King's nob. King getting
ell home on the ribs. After some sharp ding-dong
xchanges - in the close, both down.

Heenan first up, both very confident. After a good
deal of sparring, Heenan who was very active on his legs,
made his left on the right ear, and received heavily on the
ribs from King's left mawley, when Heenan dashed out
a stinger, and floored his man.

5—On coming up King showed a "mouse" on the left
eye, which pretty clearly showed Heenan's mawleys had
been very busy. The men having now warmed to their
work, commenced in earnest, and some good fighting
ensued, Heenan again putting on the ruby. After a few
good exchanges on the mouth and ribs, King dropped a
stinger on the nob, who, in return, received heavily on the
canister. A struggle to the rop s, when both were down.

6. King up gamely, but rather slow to time. On
getting together, Heenan had much the best of the fighting, and landed on the cheek and bread basket, left and
right, with beautiful precision, when King fell in his own
corner.

7.—Heenan after a short delay got his left heavily on
King's mug, and got away. King tried to return the
compliment, but was cleverly stopped. A close, both
down.

8—Heenan lugged away with his right at the mug.
This followed by some sparkling exchanges. King making
free with his opponent's nob, on which he repeatedly
planted both mawleys, drawing the claret most freely.

To particularise 9, 10, 11 and other rounds would be
only tedious, being nearly all in favour of Heenan.

The fight proceeded on after the same style until the finish
of the battle (occupying $\frac{1}{2}$ hour) when the sponge was
thrown up on the part of J. HEENAN and T. KING
was hailed the winner, amidst loud cheers from his friends
and patrons.

10 | 12 | 1863.

Printed at the 'Catnach Press," by W. S. FORTEY, Monmouth Court, Seven Dials. The
Oldest and Cheapest House in the World for Ballads (4,000 sorts), Children's Books, Song Books,

LIBRARIES. This picture shows the Reading Room of the British Museum library. Many private libraries were put together to make this huge library. It is still growing today, because a copy of every new book published in England has to be sent there. When the library first opened, no one could use it without being recommended by a peer, Member of Parliament, or judge. It was not much use for ordinary people. After 1850, free public libraries were opened in most cities and towns.

CUT-PRICE BOOKS. The picture opposite shows one of the sights of London in the early 19th century. It is the famous "Temple of the Muses," a huge cut-price bookshop. It had a sign outside: "The cheapest bookshop in the world." You can imagine how glad people were to buy books cheaply. The normal price for a book could keep a poor family in meat for a fortnight, or in candles for a month. The picture above it shows another way to buy cheap books which is still a great pleasure— buying them from second-hand bookshops.

BOOKS AND RAILWAYS. The reign of Queen Victoria saw the start of the railway age in Britain. More and more people travelled by rail between the cities and towns. Booksellers began to sell cheap books at railway stations which passengers could read on long journeys. The bookstalls of W. H. Smith were opened at all main stations in London, Manchester, Liverpool and elsewhere. Above, you can see passengers buying books on the right. Notice the many advertising posters.

ADVERTISING. As more people learned to read, manufacturers realized that advertising was a good way to interest people in their products. People who designed posters used fancy letters, exciting pictures, and even poems to attract the attention of passers-by. Theatre and circus posters were printed, too. You can see one in the top picture on the opposite page. Posters were not only displayed at railway stations. The bill-sticker in the picture opposite is having trouble trying to paste his poster to the wall.

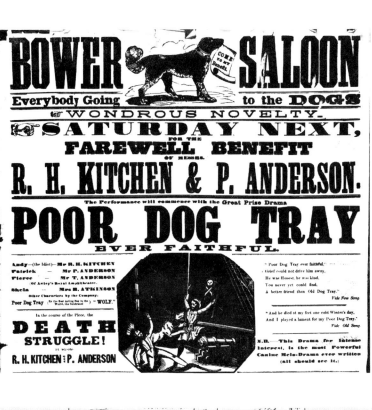

Departed is with duetee and honour
Out of this foule prisoun of this lyf?
Why grucchen heere his cosyn and his wyf
Of his welfare that loved hem so weel?
Kan he hem thank? Nay, God woot, never a deel,
That bothe his soule & eek hemself offende,
And yet they mowe hir lustes nat amende.
WHAT may I conclude of this longe serye,
But after wo, I rede us to be merye,
And thanken Juppiter of al his grace?
And er that we departen from this place,
I rede that we make of sorwes two,
O parfit joye, lastynge everemo.
And looketh now, wher moost sorwe is herinne,
Ther wol we first amenden and bigynne.
Suster, quod he, this is my fulle assent,
With al thavys heere of my parlement,
That gentil Palamon, thyn owene knyght,
That serveth yow with wille, herte, and myght,
And evere hath doon, syn that ye first hym knewe,
That ye shul, of your grace, upon hym rewe,
And taken hym for housbonde and for lord;
Lene me youre hond, for this is oure accord.

Lat se now of youre wommanly pitee;
He is a kynges brother sone, pardee,
And though he were a povre bacheler,
Syn he hath served yow so many a yeer,
And had for yow so greet adversitee,
It moste been considered, leeveth me,
For gentil mercy oghte to passen right.
THANNE seyde he thus to Palamon ful right:
I trowe ther nedeth litel sermonyng
To make yow assente to this thyng;
Com neer, and taak youre lady by the hond.
Bitwixen hem was maad anon the bond
That highte matrimoigne, or mariage,
By al the conseil and the baronage,
And thus with alle blisse and melodye
Hath Palamon ywedded Emelye;
And God, that al this wyde world hath wroght,
Sende hym his love, that it deere aboght.
For now is Palamon in alle wele,
Lyvynge in blisse, in richesse, and in heele;
And Emelye hym loveth so tendrely,
And he hire serveth al so gentilly,
That nevere was ther no word hem bitwene
Of jalousie, or any oother tene.
Thus endeth Palamon and Emelye,
And God save al this faire compaignye.
Heere is ended the Knyghtes Tale.

PRIVATE PRINTING. These people in the picture opposite are looking at an Albion handpress on display at a trade exhibition. Small printers, amateurs and artists began to use these presses because they believed that the fast printing used for books and magazines often led to careless work. They wanted a return to the hand methods of the early craftsmen-printers. The artist William Morris (1834–96) used an Albion press to print his edition of *The Canterbury Tales*. Below the press is a page from his book; it is rather like something from the Middle Ages.

PRINTING AT HOME. The picture below shows a family at home in Victorian times. Small printing presses like the one on the table were known as "parlour presses." They were sold to amateurs who took up printing as a hobby. The girl on the right is composing type by hand. Her parents are checking a finished page. Poems, visiting cards and Christmas cards were printed for fun on these little presses.

SPECIAL PRINTING

We have looked at printing with type and woodblocks, and seen the presses that were used. There are other ways of printing with different equipment. Printing with type is called letterpress printing; the type surface that carries ink is higher than the background. Now think of this the other way round. In *engraving* the lines of an *image* are cut into copper or steel. In *etching* they are eaten away by acid. Lithography is a different kind of printing invented by Alois Senefelder.

Many items were printed by engraving and lithography which could not have been done by letterpress. Christmas cards, railway tickets, paper money, stamps, posters—these are a few things printed in a special way. They tell us a lot about the tastes of the people who used them. They were often thrown away by their owners, but nowadays many people collect them as a valuable record of the past.

Today photography is used a great deal in printing. This book has been printed by film. Instead of using pieces of metal type, the letters have been photographed to make up the words in this book. This is just one way of using photography in printing.

Try to list all the different things which have been printed. If you start to collect examples of printing in a scrapbook, you will be surprised at the number you can find.

FUNERAL CARDS. Here is a funeral card from the time of Queen Anne. It was an invitation to attend someone's funeral. This card was printed from a wood-block and type in a press, just as books were. The man who made this funeral card had a lively imagination, but he was not much good as a printer. You can see that the inking was uneven and the type does not look very pleasant. Notice also that the printer has used two kinds of "s"—the old "sp" and the new "s".

ENGRAVINGS. The engraving of a theatre on the opposite page was made in the reign of George III (1760–1820). Notice that all the people and all the decoration can be clearly seen. The lines of an engraving are very delicate, and can show many details. In an engraving the lines are scratched or cut into metal. It is impossible to have such fine lines in a woodcut.

DÉCORATION DE LA SALLE DE SPECTACLE

ENGRAVING TOOLS. The artists shown opposite are carving pictures on metal plates with special tools called *burins*. The picture below them shows a very busy engraving office. The printer in front heats the engraved metal plate. Then he will ink it and put damp paper on top. The plate is passed through the rollers of the press, called a rolling press and the ink is forced onto the paper. Notice the very young apprentices who are learning the trade.

ETCHINGS. The picture below shows the evils of gambling in the time of Queen Victoria. It is a kind of print called an etching. An etcher uses acid to cut away the lines of a design. First he covers a metal plate with pitch. Then he scratches his drawing on the pitch with a needle. He puts the plate in a bath of acid and lets the acid bite into the parts of the plate exposed by the needle. The etched lines are then filled with ink, and printed like an engraving.

PRINT SELLERS. Here is an 18th century print seller. Some printers made engravings and etchings in large numbers which could be sold cheaply. Rich and poor alike bought copies of famous paintings and popular subjects to hang in their homes. This print seller carries his prints rolled up so they will not be spoiled by being folded.

80

Dr. JOHN BAGFORD,
Patron of PRINTING.

January the 2d 17⁴⁵

Printed at His Majesties Printing-Office in *Black-Fryers*.

VISITING CARDS. This visiting card was printed for John Bagford in the early 18th century. John Bagford was famous for his printing collection. His collection is now in the British Museum. The printers in the Royal Printing House made this card for him as a present. Notice the portraits of William Caxton and Johann Gutenberg. Many of the things collected by John Bagford would have been thrown away by other people. Through him, we know what early theatre tickets, pin packets and bills looked like.

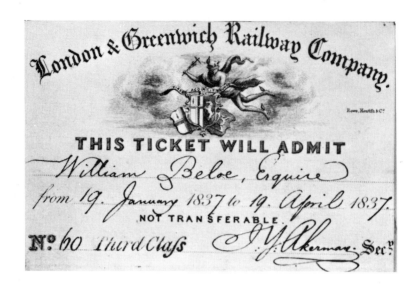

RAILWAY PRINTING. In George Stephenson's day, railway tickets were engraved; they are often very pretty. Here is one of the very first season tickets ever issued. The new railway companies needed all sorts of things to be printed—tickets, railway maps, timetables, and advertisements. George Bradshaw (1801–53), the famous Quaker printer of railway guides, also made beautiful maps by engraving.

STAMPS. Do you recognise the famous stamp? It is the first stamp ever issued, the Penny Black of 1846. It was made by Rowland Hill on a press very like an engraving press. Stamp-making has much improved since then. Nowadays the Post Office has automatic perforating and glueing machines. All the stamp designs are cleverly drawn, so that forgers cannot copy them very easily. With the invention of stamps, people found it much easier and faster to send letters by post. Above the Penny Black you can see postmen bringing sacks of mail to the General Post Office in Queen Victoria's time.

83

A ℕ°.

We promise to pay to Mr.   or bearer the Sum of
five pounds at demand, London the   day of   169

Enter'd   for the Govr. & Company of t.
                                             Bank of England

This Note to be Currant only for twelve months
And may be Checked at the Bank gratis, when desired

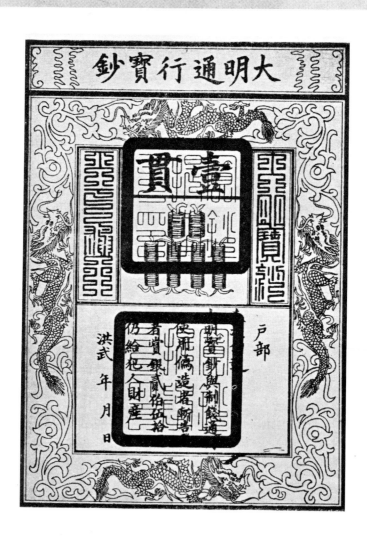

大明通行寶鈔

戶部

洪武年　月　日

LITHOGRAPHY. Alois Senefelder invented lithography in 1818. Lithography means "stone-writing". The story goes that he discovered it by accident while writing a laundry list with a greasy pencil on stone. He wetted the stone and inked it, and found that the ink stuck to the greasy pencil marks—but not to the rest of the stone. This is because grease and water will not mix. After making more experiments he worked out a way of printing, which people quickly copied everywhere. Lithography is suitable for large-scale printing, especially in colour. Big lithographic printers like this one were set up in Victorian times.

PAPER MONEY. This strange-looking object shown on the left is a Chinese banknote, printed from wood-blocks six hundred years ago. Banknotes were not printed in England until much later in the reign of William and Mary (1688–1702). The picture above the Chinese note shows a proof for one of the first English engraved banknotes. The figure of Britannica was stamped on by a seal, which was not easy to copy. This was to stop forgers from making notes of their own. If you look at a pound note today you will find a similar seal, but now it is part of the printed design.

VALENTINE CARDS. The picture opposite shows girls of Victorian times eager to see if they have received Valentine Cards on 14th February. Valentine and Christmas cards became very popular because they were cheap to print and many people could afford to buy them. Colour lithography was used to make fancy scrolls, hearts and flowers. Below the girls is a very fancy early Valentine. The first Valentines were sealed with little emblems: a pineapple meant, "You are perfect." A mushroom meant, "Suspicion".

POSTCARDS. Coloured postcards, too, were cheaply printed by lithography. Railways allowed more people to visit the seaside or foreign countries. These travellers began to send postcards to their friends. This picture shows a group of ladies on holiday in Germany writing their postcards and posting them in the box on the postman's back.

By permission of Mr. PUNCH.

'Pears' Soap

"Two years ago I used your soap, since w[...]
I have used no other."

—*Punch*, April 26th, 188[...]

ddy, what did YOU do in the Great War?

POSTERS. Posters or advertisements appeared everywhere in the late 19th century. By this time, almost
everyone could read. Posters could be printed cheaply
and in colour by lithography. A poster or advertisement
must attract attention, and this can be done in many
ways. It can be amusing like the famous Pear's Soap
advertisement, or colourful and striking like the First
World War recruiting poster.

PACKAGES. The picture below shows a canning factory at the time of the Industrial Revolution. If you look closely you can see men putting food into tin cans, sealing them and sticking on printed labels. The top picture is an early Kellogg's cornflakes packet. It looks different from the packets we know today. Labels like this are only one of the hundreds of everyday uses of printing.

LINO CUTS. Now that you have read about letterpress, woodcuts, lithography, and other forms of printing, why not make a print yourself at home? It is very easy to make prints from lino cuts or potato cuts. This picture of Brighton Pier was printed by lino by the artist Edward Bawden. Just draw a design on the lino and cut away the background with a knife. Be careful not to cut yourself or to cut away too much. Put on the colours by hand, and press a piece of paper on top. If you use a few books as a press, you should get a very good result!

TABLE OF DATES

NEW WORDS
TO REMEMBER

Almanac	Annual calendar which tells the future from the stars
Burin	Engraving tool
Chapel	A group of printers who work together
Compositor	Someone who "composes", or makes up the type letters into words, ready for printing
Edition	Form in which a book is published
Engraving	Picture printed from lines cut into a metal plate with a burin
Etching	Picture printed from a metal plate with lines cut out by acid
Folio	Large size books. The sheet of paper used for printing is folded only once
Hieroglyphics	Ancient Egyptian writing using pictures instead of letters and words
Impression	Number of copies of a book printed at one time. Also, a print made from type, a woodblock or an engraving
Industrial Revolution	General name given to all the inventions and changes in technology which took place in the late 18th and early 19th centuries
Journeymen	Skilled workmen hired and paid by the day. Every journeyman was once an apprentice and now works for a master printer

Letterpress	Printing from type
Ligature	Two or more letters of type joined together (as in Aesop)
Lithography	Printing from inked stone
Manuscript	Something written by hand
Middle Ages	Term used to describe the period roughly between the Norman Conquest and the Tudors
Mould	Hollow form in which hot metal is poured to cast type
Papyrus	Ancient writing surface prepared by Egyptians and others from the stem of reeds
Parchment	Skins of sheep and goats prepared for writing and sometimes for printing
Perfecting	Printing on both sides of a page at once
Proof	Specimen of printing used for checking
Renaissance	Term used to describe the revival of learning about 1500. From the French word meaning "rebirth"
Rotary Press	Printing machine with type mounted on cylinders. Paper is passed through the cylinders to be printed.
Scribes	Someone who copies out writing. Many monks in the Middle Ages were scribes
Type	Tiny piece of metal with a letter of the alphabet cut from it, used for printing
Typefounder	Someone who makes type by casting it in a mould
Vellum	A fine form of parchment made from calf skin

MORE BOOKS

Catchpenny Prints: Popular Engravings from the Eighteenth Century (Dover Publications, New York, 1970). This book contains a short introduction and many amusing pictures.

De Vries, L. *Little Wide-Awake: An Anthology from Victorian Children's Books and Periodicals* (Arthur Barker, 1967). This book has many pictures from children's books and a simple text.

Havercroft, R. H. *A Book is Made for You* (Harrap, new edition, 1970). The story of what happens to a book from the time it is written until the time you read it.

Kay, F. G. *Printing. It's Made Like This Series* (John Baker, 1968). For those who are interested in the technical side of printing.

Thomas, D. *The Story of Newspapers* (Methuen, 1965). A good historical account of newspapers, with fine pictures.

Tingle, R. *Let's Print.* One of the "Starting Points" series edited by Henry Pluckrose. (Evans, 1971). For younger children.

Uden, G. *The Knight and the Merchant* (Faber, 1965). A vivid story of the lives of two men, one a knight and the other a merchant—William Caxton who brought printing to England.

INDEX

PICTURE CREDITS